D0442936

Behind every
successful woman is
a substantial amount of

Copyright © 2016 by Suzy Toronto.

All rights reserved. No part of this publication may be reproduced, stored in a retrieval system or transmitted in any form or by any means, electronic, mechanical, photocopying, recording or otherwise, without the written permission of the publisher.

ISBN: 978-1-68088-062-5

Wonderful Wacky Women®

Inspiring•Uplifting•Empowering

is a trademark of Suzy and Al Toronto. Used under license.

N and Blue Mountain Press are registered in U.S. Patent and Trademark Office. Certain trademarks are used under license.

Printed in China.
2nd printing: 2017

⊛ This book is printed on recycled paper.

This book is printed on paper that has been specially produced to be acid free (neutral pH) and contains no groundwood or unbleached pulp. It conforms with the requirements of the American National Standards Institute, Inc., so as to ensure that this book will last and be enjoyed by future generations.

Blue Mountain Arts, Inc.
P.O. Box 4549, Boulder, Colorado 80306

Behind every successful woman is a substantial amount of *Chocolate*

Suzy Toronto

Blue Mountain Press™
Boulder, Colorado

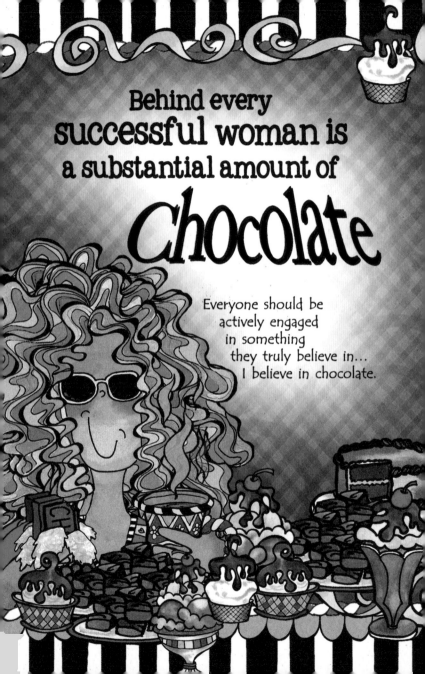

As a matter of fact,
I believe in excessive amounts
of really good, rich, dark chocolate.
Besides, I can't think of anything
that's not immoral or illegal
that makes me as happy.

And now they say
it's actually good for us!
So there you go...
it's a green light,
a legitimate excuse,
PERMISSION FROM GOD
to eat all the chocolate you want!

If It's Not Chocolate, It's Not Breakfast

Not everyone is a morning person.
For some of us, it takes far more than
the promise of a steaming cup of coffee
or a hearty, robust breakfast
to drag us out of bed.
It takes chocolate...
lots and lots of chocolate.

To this end, some brilliant chef invented the muffin.
No, I'm not eating a cupcake for breakfast.
It's a muffin... with a little frosting... and a few sprinkles.
And everyone knows muffins are good for you.
They are chock-full of good stuff like
eggs, milk, butter, and flour.
And now, scientists have discovered that
cacao beans are bursting with antioxidants —
making chocolate practically a health food.

So the breakfast dilemma is now solved.
Just crawl out of bed, lick off the icing,
and enjoy your healthy "muffin."

(You're welcome!)

©Suzy Toronto

STOP What You're Doing and Start Living!

Have you ever noticed how few people really live their lives? They just seem to go through the motions, always waiting for next week, next month, or next year to give them a sense of relief.

© Suzy Toronto

It's a trap that's far too easy to fall into.
(Oh yeah, I know you've been there.
I was the wild-haired, wacky woman
right next to you, running around
like a chicken with her head cut off,
cramming chocolate into her mouth
faster than you can say "hot fudge sundae.")

So right this very second,
stop what you're doing and start living.
Let go of the chaos and choose to
fully embrace every minute of your life.
Proclaim today as your day and this
very instant as your moment for the taking.
This day will never come again.
Next week will still come,
deadlines will fly by,
and appointments will come and go,
but by tomorrow...
today will be gone forever.

So take a deep breath,
pop in a yummy piece
of chocolate,
and LIVE!

Wonderful Wacky Words...
Believe in Yourself

Don't be afraid to dip your French fries in your chocolate shake  Your future does not lie in front of you... it lies deep inside you  You are the architect of your own destiny  When life gives you a second chance, take it  You serve the world best by serving and lifting others  Think big... if that doesn't work, think bigger

© Suzy Toronto

Don't let your frame of mind
frame you in  Embrace Plan B
as a marvelous opportunity Trust
your crazy ideas It's okay to
color outside the lines Live like
you mean it Nobody can make
you feel inferior without your
permission Let your creativity
run wild Reach outside your
comfort zone Let your dreams
take flight It's time to create
the life you've always imagined

Life Is Short...
Go for the Cupcakes!

Being a practical person is a good thing.
In a world of crippling debt,
overindulgence,
and instant gratification,
tightening your belt a bit
is wise and prudent.
But extremes in either direction
are not the answer.
Self-deprivation can be
just as damaging as
going the opposite way,
to the point where
we lose our appetite
to grow and to
experience and
enjoy life.

© Suzy Toronto

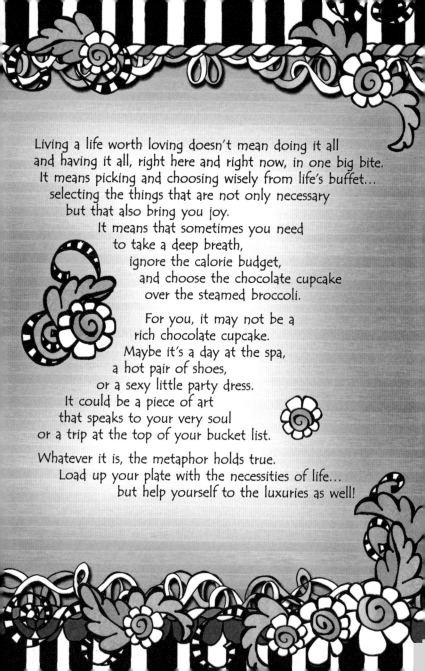

Living a life worth loving doesn't mean doing it all
and having it all, right here and right now, in one big bite.
It means picking and choosing wisely from life's buffet...
selecting the things that are not only necessary
but that also bring you joy.
It means that sometimes you need
to take a deep breath,
ignore the calorie budget,
and choose the chocolate cupcake
over the steamed broccoli.

For you, it may not be a
rich chocolate cupcake.
Maybe it's a day at the spa,
a hot pair of shoes,
or a sexy little party dress.
It could be a piece of art
that speaks to your very soul
or a trip at the top of your bucket list.

Whatever it is, the metaphor holds true.
Load up your plate with the necessities of life...
but help yourself to the luxuries as well!

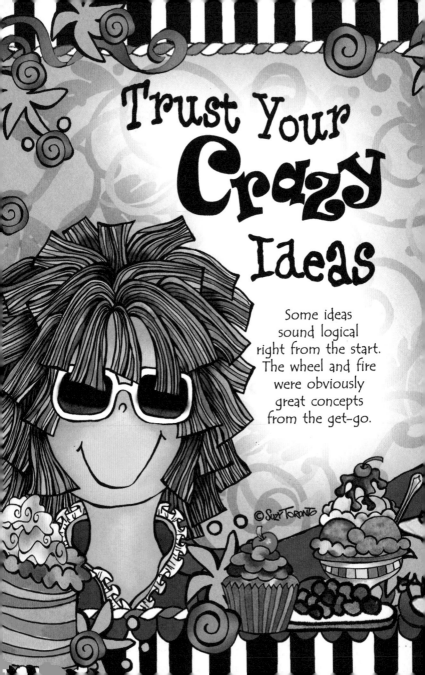

Trust Your Crazy Ideas

Some ideas
sound logical
right from the start.
The wheel and fire
were obviously
great concepts
from the get-go.

© Suzy Toronto

But I wonder who first
watched a chicken lay an egg
and said, "Hey, let's eat that!" Yuck!
That was probably met with some
skepticism. At the time, no one had visions
of chewy fudge-filled cookies, dense tortes,
silky mousses, or delicate chocolate soufflés.

New ideas always encounter criticism and
opposition. But remember, most inventions
begin in somebody's basement by one
man or woman with a vision.
The key to success is to
believe in yourself and persevere.

So trust your crazy ideas.
They could change
the world!

French Silk Chocolate Headache

One of my besties and I decided to skip lunch one day while at a workshop and split a piece of this decadent dessert instead. Forty-five minutes later, all that richness in our empty tummies gave us both splitting headaches. But it was so delicious, we decided it was worth every single bite!

- A bunch of chocolate sandwich cookies
- 1 prepared 8-inch pie shell, baked and cooled
- ½ cup (1 stick) unsalted butter, softened
- ¾ cup sugar
- 1 ounce (1 square) unsweetened chocolate, melted and cooled
- 1 teaspoon vanilla extract
- 2 large pasteurized eggs
  For garnish: whipped cream and pecans

Smash up enough cookies to fill the bottom of the baked pie shell, pressing firmly. You don't need to add anything else because the frosting between the wafers will hold it all together.

In a medium bowl, cream butter and sugar with an electric mixer until very light and fluffy — the longer you beat it, the better. Mix in chocolate and vanilla extract until blended. Now add eggs one at a time: beat the first one at medium speed for 5 minutes; then add the second one and beat for an additional 5 minutes. Do not cut this step short. Dump the whole mixture into the prepared crust. Chill for 2 hours.

Top with whipped cream and pecans.

© Suzy Toronto

Some Days You Just Have to Act "As If..."

...you know, "as if" everything is okay, "as if" everything is normal, and "as if" the world were simply covered in a comforting layer of rich chocolate (despite the fact that you know it's just an act). Some people call it "fake it till you make it," but I like to think of it more as acting with faith.

© Suzy Toronto

It's about believing in something you
can't see or touch. It's about reaching deeper
into yourself than ever before to find your true
strength and courage... even if they're right alongside
doubt and fear. And it's about ignoring
the voices around you that tell you to give up.

Think of it this way:
What if just around the next corner
the world's largest chocolate bar
is waiting for you?
What if the rainbow's end
is just around the bend,
its pot of gold filled with chocolate coins?
What if you act "as if" for just one more minute?
This is not the time to wimp out and be a health nut.
This is the time to press forward with faith.
This is the time to put on your game face
and act "as if" nothing were impossible.
When you do, you will stand tall
with conviction and pride, knowing you have
finally created the life you've always imagined.

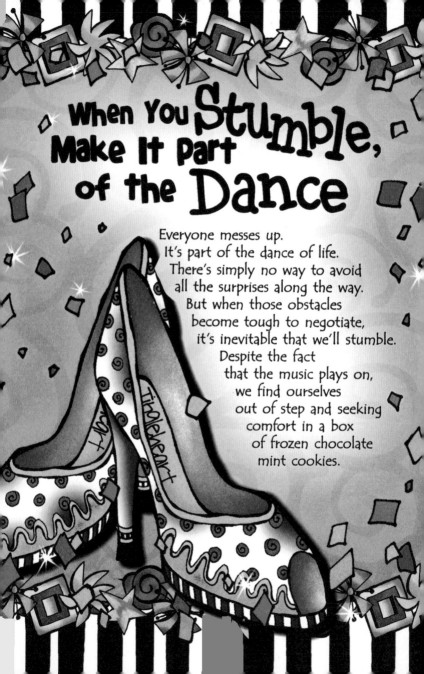

When You Stumble, Make It part of the Dance

Everyone messes up.
It's part of the dance of life.
There's simply no way to avoid
all the surprises along the way.
But when those obstacles
become tough to negotiate,
it's inevitable that we'll stumble.
Despite the fact
that the music plays on,
we find ourselves
out of step and seeking
comfort in a box
of frozen chocolate
mint cookies.

That's when creativity and adaptability
become our most valuable, lifesaving virtues.
They help us muster up the courage to carry on
and simply act as if it were all part of the show...
even though behind the scenes
our pride may have been battered and bruised.
Without offering apologies,
excuses, or explanations,
we discover that it's just a matter of
continuing onward with all our heart and soul
as if our lives depended on it.

So the next time you stumble,
smile at the crowd,
kick up your heels, and dance a jig!
The moment you embrace it as your own,
no one will know
it's not part of *your* dance.

© Suzy Toronto

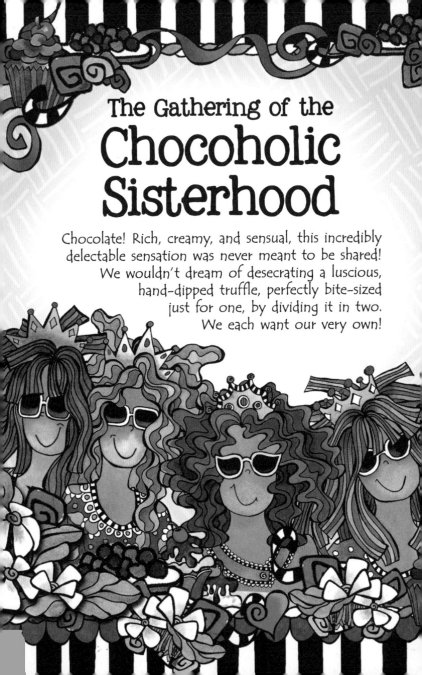

The Gathering of the
Chocoholic Sisterhood

Chocolate! Rich, creamy, and sensual, this incredibly delectable sensation was never meant to be shared! We wouldn't dream of desecrating a luscious, hand-dipped truffle, perfectly bite-sized just for one, by dividing it in two. We each want our very own!

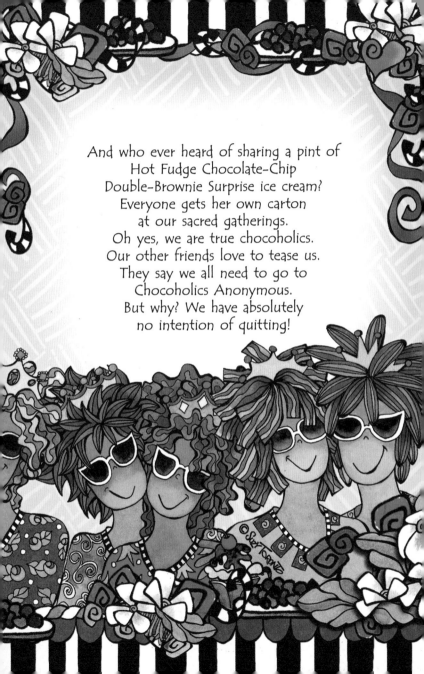

And who ever heard of sharing a pint of
Hot Fudge Chocolate-Chip
Double-Brownie Surprise ice cream?
Everyone gets her own carton
at our sacred gatherings.
Oh yes, we are true chocoholics.
Our other friends love to tease us.
They say we all need to go to
Chocoholics Anonymous.
But why? We have absolutely
no intention of quitting!

Wonderful Wacky
Reasons to Love
Chocolate

Chocolate is nature's way of making up for Mondays 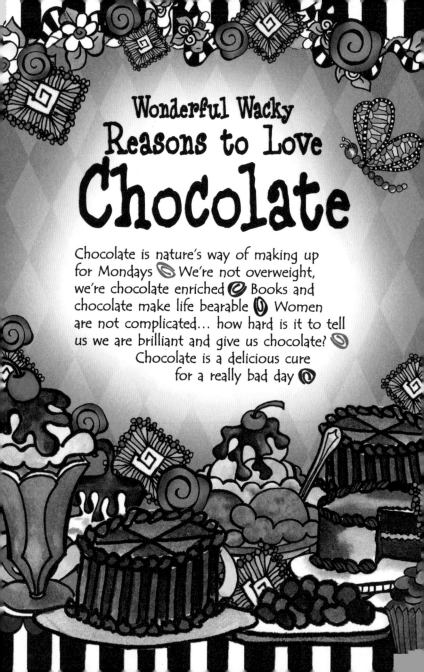 We're not overweight, we're chocolate enriched Books and chocolate make life bearable Women are not complicated… how hard is it to tell us we are brilliant and give us chocolate? Chocolate is a delicious cure for a really bad day

The calories in chocolate are reduced
to zero if no one sees you eating it
If life had a flavor, it would be chocolate
The taste of rice cakes significantly
improves when dipped in chocolate
Chocolate is to women what duct tape
is to men: it fixes everything Coffee
makes it possible to get out of bed...
but chocolate makes it worthwhile
No one's last words were ever
"I wish I'd eaten less chocolate"
With all my heart and soul
I believe in the pursuit of
life, liberty, and really
good chocolate

©Suzy Toronto

SUZY'S SOUTHERN CHOCOLATE SOUR CREAM CAKE

If you're going to blow a diet, make it worth every bite. This cake is so good that you'll want to throw a party just for an excuse to bake it. (Personally, I think it's better the second day, so whip it up the day before if possible.)

- ¾ cup unsweetened cocoa powder
- 1¾ cups sugar, divided
- 4 large eggs, 3 of them separated
- ½ cup milk
- ½ cup (1 stick) butter or margarine
- 2 cups all-purpose flour, sifted
- 1 teaspoon baking powder
- 1 teaspoon baking soda
- ½ teaspoon salt
- 1 teaspoon vanilla extract
- 1 cup sour cream

Preheat oven to 350 degrees. Grease the bottoms of three 8-inch cake pans and line with parchment paper.

In a medium saucepan over low heat, combine cocoa powder, ¾ cup sugar, 1 egg yolk, and milk. Cook, stirring until thickened. Cool.

In a large bowl, cream butter with an electric mixer until light and fluffy; add remaining 1 cup of sugar and beat until well blended. Add 1 egg and 2 egg yolks. Mix well.

In a medium bowl, combine flour, baking powder, baking soda, and salt. Stir dry ingredients alternately with sour cream into butter mixture. Add vanilla extract and cocoa mixture. In a medium bowl, beat remaining 3 egg whites with an electric mixer until stiff, and fold into batter. Pour batter evenly into the pans. Bake for 30 to 35 minutes. Turn cakes out onto cooling racks and peel off parchment paper. Cool.

Chocolate Butter Frosting
- ¾ cup (1½ sticks) butter, softened
- 6 cups sifted powered sugar (approx. 1½ lbs.)
- 1 dash salt
- 2 teaspoons vanilla extract
- 5 ounces (5 squares) unsweetened chocolate, melted
- ¼ cup sour cream, divided

In a large bowl, cream butter with an electric mixer; gradually mix in powered sugar. Add salt, vanilla extract, melted chocolate, and about 3 tablespoons of sour cream. Beat until smooth and spreadable, adding more sour cream if necessary.
Frost cooled cake, and lick the bowl clean.

© Suzy Toronto

Don't Let Your Frame of Mind Frame You In

Have you ever felt like diving face-first into a chocolate fountain? Who needs dainty skewers and fancy fruit for dipping? And who cares if there are people everywhere? We're talking about luscious, velvety, cascading chocolate!

Most of us have crazy thoughts like that, but we don't act on them. Our frame of mind frames us in. It dampens our growth, stamps out our creativity, and wreaks havoc with our imagination.

© Suzy Toronto

Daring to be wacky means
stepping out of our comfort zones,
taking a chance, and creating a life worth loving.
Sure, it's risky — but so what?
Being a wacky woman means following your heart.
You don't have to be obnoxious or extreme;
just be willing to step outside the box,
let go of your doubts, and grab hold of
the first opportunity that comes your way.
Take music lessons. Go back to school.
Make friends with an old rival.
Volunteer for a charity. Run a race.
Adopt a mutt. Try out for a play.
Join a yoga class.
The results will amaze you.
You're never too old,
too young, too rich,
or too poor to just *do it*.
Ready? Set. Go!

Suzy's Secret
Mint Chocolate-Chip
Ice Cream with
Hot-Fudge Sauce Party

This is my most favorite, very secret recipe in the history of forever for serious girlfriend bonding. When followed exactly, it has never failed to throw me and my besties into fits of irrepressible laughter, hugging, and just simply having fun.

* 1 jar of your favorite outrageously delicious hot-fudge sauce (Do not buy the cheap stuff!)
* 1 half-gallon of the best quality mint chocolate-chip ice cream you can possibly afford

Call your best friend and invite her over. While she is en route, grab a spoon and eat a well out of the center of the half-gallon container. Dump the entire jar of hot-fudge sauce into the well. Get two long-handled iced-tea spoons ready. (They're more fun to eat with.)

When your friend arrives, tell her how much you love and appreciate her, swear her to secrecy, and then dive in. Remember, calories don't count if you don't tell anyone.

Sit, laugh, cry, hug, talk, and eat — oh… and have a bite for me.

© Suzy Toronto

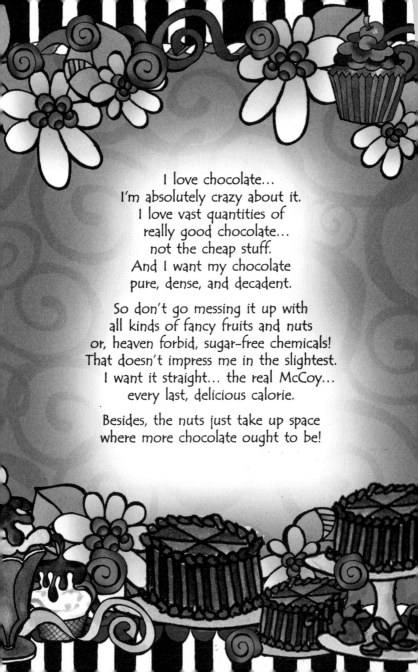

I love chocolate...
I'm absolutely crazy about it.
I love vast quantities of
really good chocolate...
not the cheap stuff.
And I want my chocolate
pure, dense, and decadent.

So don't go messing it up with
all kinds of fancy fruits and nuts
or, heaven forbid, sugar-free chemicals!
That doesn't impress me in the slightest.
I want it straight... the real McCoy...
every last, delicious calorie.

Besides, the nuts just take up space
where more chocolate ought to be!

The Common Core of Chocolate

There has been so much talk lately
about the new ways of teaching our youth.
These methods confound anyone who ever
went to school when we still memorized
times tables and learned cursive writing.

Enter the new generation.

What once seemed simple is now confusing.
They tell us the new method simplifies
problem solving and makes
everything easier to understand.

© Suzy Toronto

Well, the new fandangled logic has now entered the world of chocolate. And finally, wonder of wonders, the new curriculum makes perfect sense. Let me explain:

1. Chocolate comes from cacao beans.
2. Cacao beans come from cacao trees.
3. That makes them a plant.
4. Chocolate is a salad.

OK, it may not make sense to everyone, but it works for me, and I'm going with it.

So... wanna join me for a salad?

Do not take the advice
of those old sages
and wait until you can
"walk confidently
in the direction of your dreams."
If you do, you'll never take the first step.
Instead, leap and learn to fly on the way down.
(And for heaven's sake, don't wait
until you lose ten pounds!)

Now is the time to jump in with both feet...
arms flailing, hair flying, and screaming at
the top of your lungs, "I can do this!"
You don't have to believe it...
you just have to do it.

Start now...
right after you have
a big bite of chocolate!

Dip It in Chocolate
...It'll Be Fine!

If there's one thing I can depend on in my wild, wacky, upside-down, inside-out world, it's my undying love for chocolate. It's the most delicious relationship I've ever had!

© Suzy Toronto

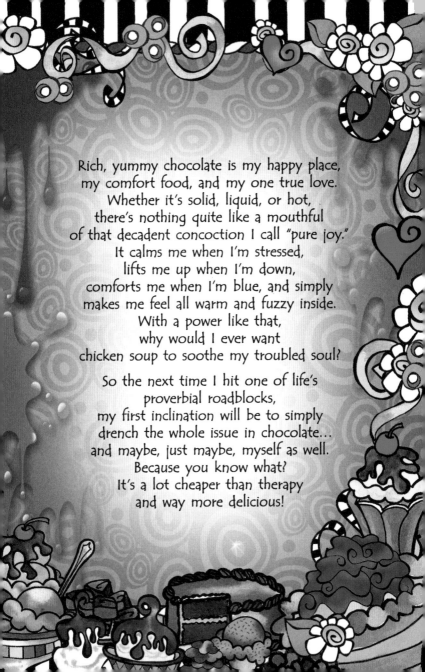

Rich, yummy chocolate is my happy place,
my comfort food, and my one true love.
Whether it's solid, liquid, or hot,
there's nothing quite like a mouthful
of that decadent concoction I call "pure joy."
It calms me when I'm stressed,
lifts me up when I'm down,
comforts me when I'm blue, and simply
makes me feel all warm and fuzzy inside.
With a power like that,
why would I ever want
chicken soup to soothe my troubled soul?

So the next time I hit one of life's
proverbial roadblocks,
my first inclination will be to simply
drench the whole issue in chocolate...
and maybe, just maybe, myself as well.
Because you know what?
It's a lot cheaper than therapy
and way more delicious!

About the Author

So this is me… I'm a tad wacky and just shy of crazy. I'm fiftysomething and live in the sleepy village of Tangerine, Florida, with my husband, Al, and a big, goofy dog named Lucy. And because life wasn't crazy enough, my eightysomething-year-old parents live with us too. (In my home, the nuts don't fall far from the tree!) I eat far too much chocolate, and I drink sparkling water by the gallon. I practice yoga, ride a little red scooter, and go to the beach every chance I get. I have five grown children and over a dozen grandkids who love me as much as I adore them. I teach them to dip their French fries in their chocolate shakes and to make up any old words to the tunes they like. But most of all, I teach them to never, ever color inside the lines. This is the Wild Wacky Wonderful life I lead, and I wouldn't have it any other way. Welcome to my world!